Josephine Walcott

World of Song

Josephine Walcott

World of Song

ISBN/EAN: 9783744652636

Printed in Europe, USA, Canada, Australia, Japan

Cover: Foto ©Thomas Meinert / pixelio.de

More available books at **www.hansebooks.com**

WORLD OF SONG.

CAMBRIDGE:
Printed at the Riverside Press.
1878.

Copyright, 1878,
By JOSEPHINE WALCOTT.

To

CALIFORNIA — THE GOLDEN EMPIRE,

SO GRACIOUSLY RESPONSIVE TO TOIL,

SO SOFTLY WOOING TO REPOSE,

This Volume

IS REVERENTLY AND TRUSTINGLY DEDICATED.

To

CALIFORNIA — FAIR SOVEREIGN,

THAT SWAYS THE REGAL SCEPTRE OF SUNSHINE AND CALM SEAS;

WHOSE BURNISHED WINDS RIPPLE LIGHTLY

AMONG THE PAGES AS I WRITE;

BELIEVING IN THE HONOR AND NOBILITY OF HER SONS AND HER DAUGHTERS,

AND IN THE ULTIMATE GREATNESS OF HER DESTINY,

I DEDICATE MY FUTURE,

WITH ITS WEALTH OF HOPES AND AIMS.

THE AUTHOR.

PREFACE.

It is only at the earnest solicitation of many friends, that the author has been induced to gather in volume these fugitive fragments that her poetic genius has flung upon the world of literature, never recking what fate awaited them.

These heart-echoes, too often in sadly sweet refrain, but sometimes in joyous pulsings, responsive to nature's glad volition, were the inevitable and spontaneous utterances of her inner life; and those who know and love her best fear not that these soul-breathings will be less potent to soothe and sustain the weary, to inspire to tender, sacred thought, or noble, constant endeavor, than when in fugitive wandering they attracted many a touching tribute and heartfelt response from those who knew her not, only as kindred souls recognize and answer each other.

And well we know that those whose inmost thoughts delight to linger among the sublime, the beautiful and true, in this tender volume will find safe pilot into the World of Song.

H. M. B.

CONTENTS.

	PAGE.
CALIFORNIA	7
THE SYCAMORE TREE	9
THE LOST FRIEND	11
ROSES	13
THE PALM TREE	16
A DAY OF PROMISE	18
DEFEATED	20
SUNDERED	22
OVER THE SEA	26
SUMMER	28
SOUTHERN DREAMING	31
ONLY SEEDS	33
THE CHOSEN FRIEND	36
BY THE SEA	38
SANTA BARBARA	40
LILIES	42
FORECAST	44
FULFILLED	47
SUNDOWN	49
BEYOND THE NIGHT	52
LITTLE NELL THAT DIED	54
ENCHANTMENT	55
ELFIE GRAY	57
BY THE SEA	58
THE HAUNTED HEART	61
LIFE	63
SING TO ME, DARLING	64
ONWARD	66
I REMEMBER	68
THE CHIEFTAIN'S REVENGE	70

THE BATTLE WON	73
DRIFTING AWAY	76
ON NEW YEAR'S EVE	78
REQUIEM	81
LENT	83
EASTER	86
EASTER	88
CHRISTMAS	90
NEED OF ME	93
MY ANGEL VISITANT	95
REVERIES	97
REPROACH	99
ANNA SNOW	101
ALMOST	103
AFTERWARD	105
THE WEDDED LIFE	107
CHRISTMAS HYMN	109
TRUST	111
MY HEAVENLY FRIEND	113
RECOMPENSE	115
WHERE CAN THE SOUL FIND REST	117
UNDER THE SNOW	119
COMPENSATION	121
A DAY OF GLADNESS	122
DEAD	124
ONE	126
THE LOST LOVE	128
RESPITE	130
THE USES OF LIFE	132
ANSWERED	134
PERADVENTURE	136
THERE IS NO LOSS	138
UNUTTERED THOUGHTS	141
PROPHECY	143
ON THE SUMMIT	145
STRANDED	148
DESTINY	150
BEAUTIFUL LINKS	152
IMMORTAL LIFE	154
"IS IT UP HILL ALL THE WAY?"	156

WORLD OF SONG.

CALIFORNIA.

Follow the dreams of thy youth."
SCHILLER.

It haunted me amid the sunrise splendor —
  A golden dream of sunset and of thee;
'Mid dusky woodlands or by shining rivers,
  On granite hilltops, or by Orient sea.

I dreamed of palms, beneath the dark-leaved maple;
  Of orange groves, among the Northern pine;
In lands aflame with gorgeous Autumn glories,
  I roamed in dreams 'mid Southern fig and vine.

I heard the mighty storm sob through the forest,
  Or solemn anthems peal through arch and aisle;

And dreams of thee, sweet world of song and sonnet,
  With strange deep longings thrilled my soul the while.

I dreamed of calms, where wind-harps hush forever,
  In tender cadence of undying love;
And sea winds waft a sweet, unspoken story,
  And tender skies eternal shine above.

Fair land of sunset, my young dream fulfilling, —
  For I have followed thy sweet thought, O youth!
And from thy purple hills and golden heather
  Shall sing new bards, with grand prophetic truth.

Thy seas shall bear white ships to safest harbor;
  Thy valleys yield sweet wealth of fruit and grain;
Thy regal hillsides glow with purple vintage;
  Thy tender skies fall summer sun and rain.

Thy sons shall be as gods of classic story;
  Thy regal daughters noble, fair, and strong.
From thy new world shall rise immortal heroes,
  O golden land of labor, art and song!

THE SYCAMORE TREE.

I SEE it waving in the rosy sunrise,
   Its large leaves glittering with the fragrant dew,
While purple shadows linger 'mid the branches
   Where shy birds nestle all the dim night through.

And from the languid calms of tropic islands,
   And spicy zones that flush the sunset shore,
To burning skies its royal crest uplifting,
   In kingly grandeur stands the Sycamore.

I see it tossing in the noontide splendor,
   A cool, wide emerald in the sunlit air, —
A dim, rich twilight through the golden glimmer
   Of odorous heats and tropic noonday glare.

While balm winds sleep among the sanded caverns,
   While billows swoon upon a slumbering sea,
And golden heats along the brown swards quiver,
   I seek thy cool retreat, O royal tree.

THE SYCAMORE TREE.

At twilight, when the gorgeous day is waning,
  And gradual shadows tinge the distant hill,
Its dreamful silence lulls the soul to visions,
  And wild, sweet fancies through the starlight thrill.

And eagerly I lean and wait and listen,
  To ancient myth and strange, wild Indian lore,
And waiting oft, I read unwritten pages,
  The mystic volumes of the Sycamore.

I see the phantom of unstoried ages,
  I list the chorus of unuttered things:
In dumb battalions march forgotten heroes,
  From fated realms of unrecorded kings.

In solemn splendor moves the vast procession,
  In deathless glory sweep the vanished years,
With mighty hosts of loyal souls uprisen
  In deathless triumph through the swinging spheres.

O wild, weird Sycamore, wave on forever, —
  Thou swordless monarch of unbounded zones:
Reveal thy legends of forgotten ages, —
  Thy fated sovereigns of long buried thrones.

THE LOST FRIEND.

The night is gone. Day followeth after night.
Thou be my day — I folded in thy light.
Love to love answers where thy smile may be;
   Wilt thou not smile on me?

Lo, far in heaven the orb of day is hung,
And, with sweet sound, the leaves by zephyrs
  swung;
Leaf to leaf replies; bee hums unto bee;
   Wilt thou not talk with me?

The pine trees, crooning low, fling odors sweet;
The brook leaps by, some brighter brook to
  meet;
Bloom to bloom answers, fairer grows the lea;
   Wilt thou not come with me?

What of the night? Night calleth for the stars;
The lilies sleep beneath the moonbeam's bars:
Star to star answers; I call thee to be
   Moonbeam and star to me.

And what of song? The wind-harp, swept at night,
One soul enchanted by some strange delight,
So sweet, so pure, so glad, as song may be;
    Be thou a song to me.

Prince of the storm, fling out your banners gray;
Lock out the stars that mock my lonely way.
Yet not one fear, if I may wait by thee;
    Couldst thou not wait with me?

Ah me! My day, my star, my song is fled;
The leaf, the bud, the tender bloom is dead,
And only memory drifting back to me;
    Thou couldst not live for me.

ROSES.

Over the summer sweetness, —
  Swooning to deep repose,
Crowning the golden splendor, —
  Bloometh the rose.

Over the purple silence, —
  Lofty, wide, and afar,
Filling the infinite spaces, —
  Shineth a star.

Over the rosy goblet,
  Thrilling with life's new wine,
We quaffed a joy together,
  Almost divine.

Over the summer splendor, —
  Golden and amethyst, —
Quenching the light and glory,
  Lies autumn mist.

Roses withered and dying, —
  Out in the scentless morn,

I clasp with white hands bleeding,
  Only a thorn.

Over the gulfs of silence,
  Folded with pall and shroud,
I see through starless midnight,
  Only a cloud.

Out of my life has vanished
  Something too deadly sweet;
Something broken and wasted
  Lies at my feet.

Something is lost forever
  Out of the great, blank earth, —
Souls that were not begotten
  Into new birth.

Words forever unspoken, —
  Deeds forever undone, —
Who has peace everlasting,
  Under the sun?

Who has gift of perfection,
  Peerless forever with youth?
Who in ultimate ages,
  Absolute truth?

Seedtime, harvest, and vintage,
  Blossom, fruitage, and grain, —
Love is ever and ever
  Sweetest of pain.

Years roll over and under,
  Love is a pitiful sweet, —
Roses withered and scentless,
  Dead at my feet.

THE PALM TREE.

In new, glad lands, — by fair, relenting seas,
  Of golden poppies and of golden corn,
The stately Palm Tree — queen of sunset trees —
  A regal crown lifts to the rosy morn;
    So grandly fair, beneath the crescent skies,
    It holds a pledge of some new Paradise.

Amid strange perfumes of the languid noons,
  The sleepy birds are faint with tropic heat;
The royal Palm Tree, by the still lagoons,
  With low, cool shadows, wooes my lingering feet.
    'Mid daffodils of gleaming, dusky gold,
    In new, sweet dreams, I half forget the old.

I dream of one so lordly fair and sweet, —
  And all the world is one vast, dim eclipse, —
A summer heaven lies at my waiting feet,
  A thrill of kisses lingers on my lips.
    The passion flower is swooning with the rose,
    And bird and bee are lost in deep repose.

THE PALM TREE.

I haunt the shadows of this loyal tree,
  The light wind ripples through the golden calm,
A great, sweet passion holds the sky and sea,
  I wait beneath the royal crown and palm;
    And all the land grows dark with spear and leaf,
    And golden poppies blend with golden sheaf.

O pride of the World, and love of the Sun!
  Thy emerald groves, O beautiful Palm,
Shall be my rest forever, when won,
  And my soul is filled with a deep, sweet calm.
    I know this tree shall wave immortal fair,
    In deathless beauty through heaven's sacred air.

O land of the Palm, and land of the Sun!
  All sandaled with gold and tasseled with wheat,
With fig tree and vine when labor is done,
  And shadow of Palms through glimmering heat,
    I have no love from thee, sweet land, apart,
    My love of loves is in thy great, warm heart.

A DAY OF PROMISE.

O DAY so languidly sweet, so sweet,
   O rose of a dawn-tinted sky,
O dainty blooms that swoon at my feet,
   With bending of clover and rye,
O bright-throated birds that are singing,
Would you know, O glad breezes swinging,
   If some one should utter a sigh?

O sapphire sky and sapphire sea,
   O land of pearl and sea-blown shell,
O noble pledge of vine and tree,
   And tender pledge to me as well;
Do you know, O wild billows sighing,
O sunlight in rosy clouds dying,
   The promise that's promised to me?

O bloom on meadow, upland, and tree,
   O vintage of rosy, sweet wine,
O lowing of flocks and murmur of bee,
   In the golden summer's day shine;

Would you know, should we break the sweet
    pledges?
A serpent slides through the brown hedges,
  With cruel eyes fast upon me.

And I said: O day, so sweet, so sweet!
  I turned to the kind, rosy sky;
I knelt on the blooms that were down at my
    feet;
  The cruel, bright serpent slid by.
Were you glad, O blue skies above me,
Were you glad, O true souls that love me,
  That bright, cruel serpent went by?

The day flung a quiver of sunbeams
  Adown the sweet edges of night;
The eloquent moon and the star-gleams
  Commingled in flushes of light:
O day of sunny blown blushes,
O night of dim, starry hushes,
  I'm standing alone on the height.

DEFEATED.

The summer is royal with roses,
   The lilies are shining and tall,
I hear a sweet ripple of laughter —
   I'm coming, my love, at your call.

A glimmer of gold on the river,
   A glory of light on the sea,
A bird singing high in the arches —
   I wait your swift coming to me.

The earth is a passionate splendor,
   The sky is a shadowless blue,
The orange buds gleam through the hedges,
   The blossoms lie sweet in the dew.

The eagle skims over the mountain,
   The wind passes over the hill,
My glad heart awaiteth your summons,
   Where lilies are shining and still.

DEFEATED.

Oh, fleeter than sweet, my belovéd,
   This perfect, glad vision to me!
A shadow sweeps over the mountain,
   And darkens the river and sea.

You call, but my feet may not follow;
   The wind is a shiver of sighs;
A quiver of pain in the hollows,
   A shudder of death in the skies.

But labor is wise, and to-morrow
   The weary shall rest and be free;
And love — it is sweet, but its glory
   Has vanished forever from me.

SUNDERED.

They stood in the hush of the morning:
   She, with her calm, lifted eyes
Turned where a quiver of daylight
   Troubled the eastern skies;

He, turned where the high, crested mountains
   Flung their white pennons afar,
Flushed with an eager impatience,
   Led by a phantom star.

"You will go," she said, unfaltering,
   "In the ways untried and sweet;
You will climb the difficult mountain,
   With swift, unerring feet."

"You will wait, my darling," he answered,
   A light in his brave, brown eyes;
A chill shuddered through the morning,
   Trembling over the skies;

SUNDERED.

And over her passionless paleness
    Quivered one glance of the sun,
As over a snowy fastness,
    When the sweet, light day is done.

"I will wait," she uttered, "forever,
    My bravest, truest, and best;
I in the pure, glinted sunrise,
    You in the golden west."

"I will come, my darling," he murmured;
    "Sweetest and dearest, good-by;"
Sobs quivered into the sunrise,
    Mist swept into the sky.

His footfall, shivering the hushes,
    Thrilled the dumb air with a pain,
Transformed the glorified morning
    Like rifts of autumn rain.

He vanquished the difficult mountain,
    He stood by the sunset sea,
'Mid scents of the lush banana
    And lull of the broad palm-tree.

His face lost its marvelous grandeur,
    Altered the beautiful years,

Mocked of his fruitless endeavor,
    Tortured of hopes and fears.

But a tremulous, dawn-like picture,
    Touched with a tender sunrise,
Pure with an Orient splendor,
    Tinted his sunset skies.

And over those desolate mountains,
    Quiet and patient and sweet,
Watching and waiting forever
    Sound of his lingering feet,

While the morning burned to the noontide,
    And noonday paled to the night,
Keeping her desolate vigils,
    Sacred, cold, and white;

Till the years crept under and over,
    When lifted her troubled eyes,
Afar to the westward mountains,
    White in the pure sunrise.

"I will wait, as I told you, belovéd,
    In a sunrise glad and calm,—
Over the desolate mountains
    Wafted a prayer and a psalm.

"I am coming, darling," he answered;
   The turbulent seas grew calm;
She sleeps by the sunrise cedar,
   He by the sunset palm.

OVER THE SEA.

The mist has flung a gossamer net
    Over the rosy sea;
The spray a crown with diamonds set,
    Over the billows free.

Our snowy sail a glimmering crest,
    Rosy and light the sky;
The drowsy sea bird calls from her nest,
    Dreamily drift we by.

O love, we glide by glittering isles,
    Plashed by the golden sea;
My heart a mirror under thy smiles,
    I laugh or weep with thee.

The darkness comes: O vanishing light,
    Linger over the sea!
O restless night, O desolate night!
    Linger my love with me.

The day is gone, but what of the night?
  What of the dreary sea?
Our bark shall glide by hope's sweet light;
  Love the true helmsman be.

SUMMER.

O HAZY summer morn!
Soft through the misty vail of floating cloud,
    The arrowy beams of dawn
Light the calm vale, and wrap the hills in shroud
    Of silver, gleaming lace;
    Thy calm, sweet, smiling face,
    O placid summer morn!
    Through shining mist is born.

    O golden summer noon!
High on the golden hills, and glowing vale,
    The long, ripe grasses swoon;
O regal sky! O royal crownéd dale!
    Prince of the realms that be,
    Thy foot is on the sea;
    The sceptre of thy hand
    Swings through the gracious land.

    O king of land and sea!
Life follows thee, and love is in thy smile;

Ah, thou hast smiled on me.
I dream of thee, and sweet winds hush the while;
O gracious summer king!
The birds forget to sing, —
Swung to a soft repose
On some white-breasted rose.

O calm, fair, festal night!
Bride of the sun, O thou pure-thoughted moon!
O queen in garments white!
I worship at thy shrine and crave one boon.
My love is gone afar,
White moon and golden star;
He rides the wild, wide sea, —
Oh guide him safe to me.

'Tis high midsummer now,
Night thrills with sweets and odorous summer bloom;
I kiss thy shining brow,
O summer night, thou hast no ray of gloom!
O high, far, tropic sky!
O lake where lilies lie
Asleep with gem and star
Caught from the skies afar!

I sleep — O night! I dream;
Was it a sigh, was it a song I heard,
Borne on a swift star beam,
Whir of white wing of some lost, dreamy bird?
I dream, O summer night!
Or foot-falls fleet and light
Roam the brown sward with me —
O love, O light, O wide, wild sea!

SOUTHERN DREAMING.

I gaze on mountains lone and grand,
   I watch the gleam of crystal seas,
The bright waves flash the golden strand,
   The glad birds thrill through strange, fair trees ;
The winds are soft as whispered dreams,
   As low and sweet as songs of love ;
The blossoms kiss the sun's bright gleam,
   The heavens' kind arches shine above.

O dreamy land, so fair and far !
   O clasp of dimpled, shining seas !
O glance of crescent, tropic bar !
   O song of birds ! O swing of trees !
I sometimes dream the odors sweet
   Are flung from far on summer gale.
The grace of childhood, fair and fleet,
   The trill of song, the flash of sail.

O beautiful bird in summer skies !
   Oh bear my dream to friends afar :

I watch the space your swift wing flies,
    As night may watch the morning-star;
Oh bear some palm from lands of dream,
    The wealth of song till then unheard;
Bear on your wings some radiant gleam
    From this fair land, O fairest bird!

My bird sweeps through the amber space,
    The tide swings in and out of sea,
The balm winds waft with dreamy grace
    The mystic song of dreams to me.
O wind, O wave, O shining sea!
    O grace of cloud! O gleam of star!
O tender past! O sweet To-Be!
    O hope so near! O rest so far!

I dream a dream so fair and calm
    Of life, of love unfed by sighs,
Of laurel-tree and crested palm
    Agleam with birds of paradise.
Where rays of Southern summer shine,
    Where life is love, and dreams are real,
With glow of song, and flash of wine,
    O poet realm! O real ideal!

ONLY SEEDS.

I ROAMED a garden marvelously fair,
   With stately palms, and graceful swaying flowers,
And silver fountains, flashing sunlit air,
   'Mid emerald calm of dreamy, perfumed bowers.

The passion flower upheld its azure cup,
   Concealing crimson drops in depths below;
The violet lifted blue eyes fearless up,
   And rose-trees swung afoam like flakes of snow.
And gentle winds crept through the sleepy flowers,
   Then wafted far with subtle, strange perfumes;
On golden pinions lightly flew the hours,
   As lightly tossed the silvery pampas plumes.

And when I thought of one in desert lone,
   Or 'mid faint languors of some weary room, —

For sadness sways life's deepest undertone, —
　　I sought to clasp for her the light and bloom.

With lightsome touch I lingered 'mid the flowers
　　To cull the sweetest and the brightest bloom,
Nor thought to heed the swift retreating hours,
　　Till twilight hung a star amid the gloom.

With fleeting steps I passed the garden wall,
　　With trembling fingers swung the fairy gate,
Through scents, and shadows of the fir-trees tall,
　　And dew-drops flashing where the moonbeams wait.

Nor feared the phantoms of mysterious night,
　　Nor flitting birds with wide white wings unfurled,
Intent to bear the incense and the light,
　　And tender glory of the summer world.

But when I reached my lonely, friendless one,
　　My clasping hands held tangled, bloomless reeds,
Though from life's waste the midnight shut the sun
　　Of summer bloom, I proffered only seeds.

But passing oft, one weary, sunset time,
  I saw the desert blossom as the rose,
With fragrant blooms, the palm-tree and the lime,
  And fair young children 'mid the sweet repose.

Thus, when we see divinely from the hills,
  Or list the strain of silvery-throated birds,
Or note the sunbeams quiver on the rills,
  Our faultless vision offers — only words.

Oh could we know some soul in silence deep
  Would feel the glory that we may not sing,
Or that our hymning stirred the weary sleep
  Of some faint hope where shadows dimly clung;

Or could we thrill some soul to heavenly meed,
  To catch the real from phantoms that but seem,
Then could we sow in joy the desert seed,
  And weave in joy the glory of our dream.

THE CHOSEN FRIEND.

Wilt thou not wake with me?
The night is rolling with the tidal sphere,
  Above the hills dilates the morning-star,
The trembling glimmer of a daylight near,
  A pledge of glory surging wide and far.

Wilt thou not watch with me?
A quiver thrills along the mountain range,
  The shadows lift in shivers all alight,
The old, glad mystery of tide and change,
  The earth is breaking from the trance of night.

Wilt thou not wait with me?
A sudden flush the wide, long seas disclose,
  A fleet is drifting to the harbor bar,
To golden calms the snowy sails uprose,
  A pledge of peace from glad, sweet lands afar.

Wilt thou not work with me?
The night is done, the dumb, long darkness past.
  Arise, O soul, with purpose high and strong!

Arise, O soul, to labors sweet and vast!
  And thrill, O earth, with light and bloom and
    song!

  Yes, thou wilt work with me;
It matters not the vigil of the years,
  The fall of stars, or shine of wearied sun,
The dumb, cold nights of waiting and of tears,
  The great unuttered and the vast undone,
Nor swing of tides upon the wide, high sea,
For thou, O Friend, wilt labor now with me!

BY THE SEA.

The night has come, and the starlight
   Falls on the restless sea,
Like a gleam of hope through the darkness
   Of a weary doubt to me.

I see the foam of the billow
   Flash like a shining rain,
Then fall into silence and shadow,
   Like the rest that follows pain.

O wonderful, beautiful billow,
   With your changing shadow and shine,
Clasping the stars in your bosom,
   I think your life is like mine!

Like mine, reaching through the darkness,
   From the restless, moaning sea,
Pleading, with a ceaseless endeavor,
   For a life that may not be.

BY THE SEA.

You clasp your mantle, O billow,
   With gems from the brow of night!
I grasp through the shadowy future
   Sweet rays of heavenward light.

O life of ceaseless endeavor!
   O wave of the troubled sea!
Star of the weary night-watch,
   Beacon of faith to me.

O heaven, with dowers of promise!
   O earth, with travail and care!
Soul of God's mighty conception, —
   Peace on the brow of despair.

I stand by the mighty ocean,
   The starlight falls on the foam,
And a feeling of rest comes o'er me,
   Like a wanderer nearing his home.

SANTA BARBARA.

Fair is she: not as a priestess supernal — fair,
  With calm, white splendor of a soul at peace;
Not as a chiseled goddess in the moveless air
  Of classic halls, or old, famed haunts of Greece;
    But young, glad beauty, so lithesome and free,
    Her garments gemmed with pearls of the sea;
    Her hair unbound to the indolent breeze,
    My beautiful queen of the sunset seas.

True is she: not as some problem difficult of old,
  That sages wrought through slow elapse of years;
Not with the dull precision of a tale oft told,
  Of tender hopes wrecked in a gulf of fears;
    But true as sunbeams that sandal her feet,
    My beautiful queen, so loyal and sweet,
    True as the light on her health-blowing hills,
    So tender her pledge, so fleet she fulfills.

Pure is she: not as a saint, so isolate and white,
  In sacred atmosphere of vestal shrine,

Where incensed tapers, waning, fling an astral
    light,
And fretted walls of alabaster shine;
    But pure with the glitter of sea-blown things,
    With silvery ripple of fount and springs,
    With balms that waft over tropical seas,
    With calms that await by evergreen trees.

Wise is she: with myth of Druid and sylvan
    fawn,
And fabled wealth of mystic Indian lore;
Her lavish olive slopes, her grain-land, and her
    corn, —
    O golden fruitage on a golden floor! —
    Her opulent breath, the fragrance of wine,
    Her sceptre the sunbeams, her helmet the
        vine,
    She lingers and dreams of princes to be,
    My beautiful queen of the sunset sea.

LILIES.

O cool, white lily! by dim rivers resting,
    Or languid blue lagoon,
Lifting thy sweet face, in solitary places,
    To fervid skies of noon.

O pure, fair lily! through thy snowy fingers
    The foam of the rivers glide;
Sunlight on thy shining forehead trembling lingers,
    Thy cool lips kiss the tide.

O cool, dim river! thy light billows cresting
    Lily pure and pale;
Moonbeams on thy silent splendors faintly quiver,
    In beauty strangely frail.

Once, when my soul was sad, with steps so weary,
    I walked the river shore,
Weaving strange dreams of weird and shadowy fancies,
    The night sang "Nevermore."

The voices of the night, the wind, the river,
    Told tales of wild unrest.
O river cold! to lie, with pale hands cross'd, forever
    Within thy quiet breast.

But lilies pure, with alabaster faces,
    Came drifting at my feet,
With dim, unearthly lights within the waxen fingers,
    And odors strangely sweet.

O peaceful lily! thou dost bear remembrance
    Of childhood's starlit land;
Saintly brows immortal lilies wreathe forever,
    Across life's troubled strand.
Thus, lily, thou dost guide my wayward dreaming
    By heavenly graces given;
With friends long passed I roam by shining rivers,
    And dream sweet dreams of heaven.

FORECAST.

Sweet is the promise of the risen morn;
   A tinge of gold illumes the eastern skies;
A faint, far star foretold the day unborn,
   With trembling rays from some far paradise.

A rose-light flushes o'er the sleepy hills;
   The tidal seas break on a tinted shore;
A new glad day the prophecy fulfills, —
   The certain outflow of the pledge before.

Now sweet the carol of the free, wild birds;
   The tender blossoms droop with shining dew;
I silent wait with thought too sweet for words,
   Perhaps to-day my dream of dreams comes true.

The perfect day swings through the gloried space;
   The trees wave wide with bright, unfolded blooms;
A golden languor fills this summer place,
   And rose leaves waft with tender, sweet perfume.

FORECAST.

There is one day so longed for and so sweet,
   The strong, wide Future folds with eager care;
Relent thy clasp, O Future! I entreat,
   And yield to-day my dream of dreams most fair.

A gentle fragrance fills the high, wide noon;
   The balmy air blows sweet across the seas;
The frail white blossoms by the long walks swoon,
   And cool, deep shadows fringe the broad palm-
      trees.

This is a forecast of the sweet To Be, —
   The golden days of beauty and of sun;
The true, glad promise of the sky and sea,
   A pledge of joy for something nobly done.

Along the 'lumined spaces of the West
   A pale, gold star is waiting for the night;
Fair as the hope that wins my soul a rest,
   With tender rays of clear, oncoming light.

The dim, wide sky is waiting for the moon;
   A stranded boat is waiting for the tide;
A sea bird calls from yonder low lagoon;
   A weary shadow wanders by my side.

Perhaps to-morrow, kinder than to-day,
  Will crown my dream so sweet and wholly fair ;
The high ideal that gilds my dim, long way
  Will find a heaven and sweet fruition there.

FULFILLED.

The golden heats have swooned among the hills;
   The dark winds throb among the slumbering
      trees;
The low, sweet music of the mountain rills
   In trembling aria joins the choral seas.

The regal hills in purple robes enfold;
   The mountains flash their moonlit crests afar;
The sea foams toss their hair of shining gold,
   And grasp their changeful robes from sky and
      star.

The weary bird has sought his covert nest,
   And trills his mate a tender, love-lade lay;
The cool dews woo the sleepy flowers to rest,
   That odorous bloomed the long, calm, golden
      day.

Here I may sit with folded, restful hands,
   The sea-blown spray ashine among my hair,

And dream the dreams of new, glad, tropic lands,
  And kiss the night that balms each day-born care.

A mystical charm hath thy song, O sea!
  You woo with a grace so tenderly sweet,
You come a conquering king unto me,
  And fling your pearls at my venturesome feet.

I wait in the tremulous hush of the night;
  The tropical winds blow sweet from afar,
Athrill with beauty of valley and height,
  Agleam with light of each scintillant star.

A hush is over the mountain and hill,
  A calm is over the beautiful sea,
A dream the glad hope of daylight fulfills,
  In tender silences coming to me.

A dream of beauty so regally sweet,
  Of love that is tenderly true and strong,
A straight, white way for my venturesome feet,
  A poet's harp for my timorous song.

SUNDOWN.

Over the shining waters
   At sunset's flush I came;
The skies a regal quiver,
   With darts of golden flame.

Far off the turreted city,
   High-roofed with gleaming spires,
Like bayonets of armies,
   Revealed by sunset fires.

Westward, and kept asunder
   By strong guard of the bay,
Green isles, like emerald crescents,
   Enzoned by fair seas lay.

I think, O luminous city!
   Saint of the crown and palm,
Unto the soulful burden,
   You waft of rest and calm.

I think, O fair cathedral!
   Turret and steepled height,

SUNDOWN.

You bear the weary laden
   A gleam of heavenward light.

I think, O beautiful island!
   Far and onward alway,
Your golden crowns high arching,
   Between the sea and the bay,

You're like some far, fair future,
   Flashes of sea between,
The present bridging ever
   The past and sweet unseen.

Musing, the golden arrows
   Vanished in dusky gloom
To ranks of dusky warriors,
   Helmet and sable plume.

Over the deep, dark waters,
   Sailless, restful, and calm,
Breath of the sea-side angel,
   Floated its healing balm.

I thought of another ocean,
   Solemn, sailless, unknown,
Wafting its viewless legions
   On to a heavenly home.

I thought of another city,
  Stainless, pure, and unseen,
A boundless, trackless ocean,
  Darkly rolling between:

The sweet, white hope that vanished,
  And the lofty, fair Ideal,
The thought we could not utter,
  O City of the Real!

BEYOND THE NIGHT.

The white fog on the bay
Like scrolls of silver lay,
And the fair stars through heaven's high azure
    swung ;
And dim isles far away,
Beyond the opal bay,
Strange incense through the cool sea-breezes
    flung.

The ocean, white and vast,
Like some pale, ghostly past,
Dim through the veil of long, uncertain years,
In might of stern repose,
Where pale the mist uprose,
Calm as a soul enfranchised from its fears.

The wind-harp swung and sighed,
Where love unuttered died,
And great souls wept o'er mighty deeds undone,
And through the years' eclipse,
Like dim, white, distant ships,
There came a voice from Victory unwon:

BEYOND THE NIGHT.

O ·doubting soul be strong!
Be patient, suffer long.
Over life's sea a new, glad morn shall rise.
And Right shall conquer Wrong,
And silence break with song,
Joy follow grief, and peace beam from the skies.

O Faith in Death's dark prison!
Come forth, the Lord is risen.
O weary hands! O restless, waning night!
O watcher by the sea!
The heavens shall answer thee, —
The day has come with glad, effulgent light.

LITTLE NELL THAT DIED.

The shadows fall soft in the gloaming,
   The winds are all hushed on the lea,
I hear, through the dull, fading twilight,
   My little Nell calling to me.
Over mountains and through the valley,
   And over the dreamy, dim sea,
Like voice of an angel is calling
   My sweet little Nellie to me.

The twilight of life is descending;
   My tresses are silver with years;
I seek out her grave in the gloaming,
   And moisten the turf with my tears.
In the glory of youth how I loved her,
   My darling, my angel, my pride;
She sleeps 'neath the old willow's shadow,
   My dear little Nellie that died.

ENCHANTMENT.

Oh sweet blow the winds the South Seas over,
  And bright are the waves that flash on the shore,
And odorous blooms of white-tufted clover
  Gleam through the gloom of the dark sycamore.

Oh dim lies the world the white stars under;
  Asleep lies the bird in emerald nest;
The beautiful night, with pinions of slumber,
  Folds the sweet world on her bosom to rest.

Asleep lies the rose, her proud heart beating
  Aloud to the zephyr, that waits with a sigh,
Her delicate breath a dainty greeting,
  O zephyr and rose! O tropical sky!

Asleep the pure lily swung by the river,
  Her jeweled hands folded white on her breast,
With marvelous dreams of a princely giver:
  Dew-drops are diamonds and moonbeams the crest.

ENCHANTMENT.

The river-god holds a reed for a quiver,
   He catches the darts that fall from the star,
A gossamer veil from mists of the river,
   And weaves of the moonbeams a bridal car.

O lily and rose! the eyes of the morning,
   Are tender and true as glance of the night,
And wonderful robes for bridal adorning
   Are woven by roseate fingers of light.

Sweet odor and bloom, starbeams and river,
   Oh gleaming of jewels, princes and crowns,
A diamond dart from a golden quiver,
   The smile of a god, a fairy's sweet frown.

Awake in thy bower, O royal roses!
   All hail to the king ascending the sea!
On crystalline throne the lily reposes,
   The wand of enchantment is wafted to thee.

ELFIE GRAY.

In the sunshine, in the shadow,
    Fairy feet astray,
Gayer than the birds in summer,
    Little Elfie Gray.

Happy all the long, glad daytime,
    Happy dreams at night;
Fairer than the buds in spring-time
    Is our household light.

In the morning, in the evening,
    Kneeling down to pray,
With her lily hands uplifted,
    Little Elfie Gray.

Happy, winning, little blessing,
    Cheering life's sad way;
Blossom of the early spring-time,
    Little Elfie Gray.

BY THE SEA.

THE sunset glory had vanished,
   And twilight tender and dim
Stole over the shining water,
   With lull of a vesper hymn.
And sobs of a nameless sorrow
   Were lost in the great, white sea,
And stars in passionless splendor
   Shone over the night and me.

And I said, O great, sad ocean!
   With billow and foam and shine,
You never have stilled the beating
   Of wearier heart than mine.
The city is strange and cruel,
   The skies are distant and dumb,
You have heard my great, white sorrow,
   And tenderly bid me come.

And I thought of the sweet, white faces,
   And long, bright, swaying hair,

BY THE SEA.

Where the pitiful, eloquent billows,
   Would utter a psalm and a prayer;
And I thought of the white souls shriven
   From sorrow, pain, and despair, —
Like a sweet, victorious anthem,
   Swept down through the aisles of air.

The desolate, long to-morrows,
   With shudder of night and sea,
Were lost in the wondrous chorus
   That floated from far to me.
And I said, O kind, sweet ocean! —
   Like one who utters a prayer —
Oh touch the dead face gently, —
   The dead, white sorrow there.

And I turned from the pitiful ocean,
   As one from a promise of rest,
The skies were distant and darkened,
   The city lamps burned in the west;
And a murmur of something too sacred
   For mortal to utter or hear,
Swept over the vast, deep ocean,
   Like joy that follows a fear.

And I said, O life! with your burden
   Of parting and passion and pain,

The sun rises out of your darkness,
   The summer blooms follow the rain;
And something to do and to suffer,
   And something to be and to share,
Is peace after great tribulation;
   And labor is worship and prayer.

THE HAUNTED HEART.

I'm sitting by the window, Genie,
  I'm musing all alone;
And with dim images are blent
  The wind's deserted tone.

The rain is falling fast, Genie,
  The gray, cold, driving rain;
And mystic forms seem wandering by
  In viewless spirit train.

There's one so meekly fair, Genie,
  With mild, religious eyes;
She drooped and faded long ago,
  As spring's pale blossom dies.

I seem to hear her voice, Genie,
  I meet her spirit-gaze;
'T is sadder now than when we met
  In childhood's happier days.

A change, a deep, dark change, Genie,
   Swept o'er her early years;
The path of love, though fair, Genie,
   Is marked by woman's tears.

Another seems to come, Genie,
   That played beneath our trees;
He left the pure, first loves of youth
   To roam the shining seas.

He'll join no more our band, Genie,
   At twilight soft and dim;
His voice is never heard, Genie,
   To chant our evening hymn.

We cannot strew his grave, Genie,
   With flowers we love so well;
He sleeps not near his boyhood's home,
   In church-yard nor in dell.

'Tis a wild and mournful tomb, Genie,
   Far down the starless deep;
A fearful thing to die at sea:
   Sweet Genie, do not weep.

LIFE.

How should I go?
With life so sweetly laden trusted me,
Still drifting surely toward the open sea;
With one pale shade forever at the helm,
Bearing me on to that mysterious realm
      I long to know?

What shall I do?
With this great gift, I may not call my own,
A strange sweet dreaming o'er my soul has flown,
As if some thrilling voice from life immortal,
With new sweet symphonies from heaven's high
   portal,
      Bore life anew.

Thus may it be.
To garner for that harvest precious sheaves,
To find the tree of life with healing leaves,
To lift the burden from some weary one,
To hear at last from Christ's kind lips, "Well
   done.
      Come unto me."

SING TO ME, DARLING.

Sing to me, darling; let light murmurs creep
Over my spirit where shadows lie deep;
Sing, and my languishing heart may grow strong,
Borne on the billows of impassioned song;
Fold me so close in your tender embrace,
Wipe the cold drops from my forehead and face;
Tear the earth laurels away from my brow,
Wreathe it with myrtle and cypress leaves now;
Bitter the chalice from earth's troubled spring,
Fold me so tenderly, kiss me and sing.

Sing to me, darling; since last we have met
Blossoms have perished and hope stars have set;
Doubt through the faith of my childhood has
    crept;
Change through the realm of these sweet years
    has swept.
Wealth cannot people the heart's solitude;
Fame on its sanctity may not intrude;
Years since we parted, care-laden and long,
Seem but a dream, while I list your sweet song.

Sing to me, darling; your voice thrills the while,
Soft as a hymn floating through the dim aisle;
Sing of the martyr, the cross, and the palm;
Chant solemn dirges, then sing a glad psalm;
Sing of the Lowly, who suffered and died;
Sing of the Holy One, long crucified;
Sing, and this burden of sorrow may be
Gems in the crown that is waiting for me.

ONWARD.

[In an excellent literary paper published in Chicago, Ill., we find a gem from the pen of CORDELIA HAVENS, concerning which the editor says: "Five years ago this charming little poem was published for the first time in the 'Home Circle.' A desire by some dear friends that it should re-enter the columns of the press induces us to republish it. Its own merits were sufficient for this object. It was first published under the lady's own signature, who has removed to the Pacific Coast and assumed the *nom de plume* of CORDELIA HAVENS. We see some of her productions in the 'Overland Monthly,' and congratulate that magazine upon the accession of such a contributor to its columns." To the foregoing we wish to add our most cordial assent. — ED. SANTA BARBARA PRESS.]

ONWARD, roll onward, O River of Time!
Bear my frail bark to a happier clime:
Faster, roll faster, ye billowy years!
Bear me away from my grief and my tears.
Cold is the breath of the pitiless blast;
Dark are the phantoms that frown from the past;
Bear me away from my fears and my pain;
Bear me away from the wind and the rain.

Onward, roll onward, O River of Life!
Take me away from my toil and my strife;

Never, oh, never, turn backward again;
Smiles have been wasted and tears wept in vain.
Strong are the rocks that heave back the sea, —
Heave back the years that return unto me.
Swift is the comet that sweeps through its track;
Years, sweep ye onward, but never turn back.

Onward, roll onward, O shuddering Tide!
I watch for thy shore on the shadowless side;
I wait for a gleam of the shimmering sand;
I long for the joys of that far distant land.
Hide those sad years in thy sheltering breast;
Bring me a dream of the weary at rest.
Mother, remember thy child on Life's sea;
Wait by the river, but come not to me.

Onward, roll onward, O pitiless years!
Bring me a rest from my toil and my fears;
The smiles and the tears I 've given to thee
Are lost mid the wrecks of life's fathomless sea.
I 'm weary of labor, I 'm weary of pain, —
They wait by the river, yet wait all in vain.
Hide them forever, their smiles and their tears, —
O River of Life, these pitiless years.

I REMEMBER.

I REMEMBER, I remember,
   How I wandered all alone,
When the young moon's pale, sweet glimmer
   On the flashing waters shone,
Where the night-bird told his story,
   'Neath the starlight dim and pale,
Where the dew-drops fell caressing
   On the blossoms weak and frail.

I remember, I remember,
   How my cheeks were bathed in tears,
As fond memory chased each vision
   Through the vista of the years;
And my eyes grew sad and dreamy,
   When the grief-drops ceased to flow,
And a darksome spell was resting
   O'er my spirit long ago.

I remember, I remember,
   From the far-off spirit land,

I REMEMBER.

Came a form of saint-like beauty,
  Beck'ning with her angel hand.
How she spoke of joys unfading,
  In the realm of purer things;
How she soothed my unveiled sorrow,
  Hov'ring on her viewless wings.

I remember, I remember,
  How my dreamy visions fled;
Yet I felt my angel mother
  Was not numbered with the dead.
And upon my spirit resting
  Came a sweet, untroubled calm,
Healing o'er each wound of sorrow,
  With its pure and holy balm.

THE CHIEFTAIN'S REVENGE.

In native pride a chieftain stood,
    The bow he held unstrung,
And sadly from his burning brow
    His broken plume he flung.

He stood and mused there long and wild
    Of the pale-face's bitter thrall,
For oft his eagle eye had turned
    To see his brother fall.

"Ere last year's moon had waned," said he,
    "The pale-face sought our land,
And they have slain my father's race,—
    The best of all my band.

"I grieved to see my kindred fall,
    As oft the foe gained ground;
And wept that e'er the stranger's foot
    Should press my father's mound.

"Once, long ago, these valleys fair,
    These forests deep and wild,

I roamed with free and careless step,
   A happy, fearless child.

"The woodman's axe and lifted arm
   Have felled those giant trees,
And spirits chant their songs no more
   Amid their whispering leaves."

Then haughty grew the chieftain's brow,
   And flashing dark his eye;
He grasped his quivering bow, and said:
   "The pale-face soon shall die."

Then ere the stars had faded,
   Or the midnight taper gleamed,
A light along the stranger's coast
   In fiery brightness beamed.

Deep wrapt within the burning shroud
   That wrathful hand had made,
The white man groaned amid the flame,
   Or struggled with the blade.

And when the rosy light of dawn
   Stole o'er the eastern main,
The black and smoking ruins
   Were smouldering on the plain.

The Indian, on a cliff near by,
  Stood gazing sad and long,
And turned in listless languor then
  To chant his own death-song.

And when another moon had shone
  Upon the ocean wave,
The night bird sung her lonely lays
  Above the chieftain's grave.

THE BATTLE WON.

It was the hushed midnight: darkness was on the sky;
The stars forgot their light, and the damp winds hurried by.
There was silence in the glen; the river lashed the shore,
When rose those fearless men to welter in their gore.
All by the river side, all down the grassy plain,
Moans of the rolling tide would mingle with the slain.
Yet fearless, calm, and brave, their banners waving high,
The federal warriors gave a shout that rent the sky.
The clouds spread like a pall, and the river ceased its moan,
A clash through the columns tall, and a heavy dying groan.

There came a thunder sound, and the fiery shells burst high;
There was blood upon the ground; there was light upon the sky.
The guns flashed on the hill; the guns flashed by the bay;
But the troops rushed onward still, like wild deer in their play.
The earth was a bloody seal; the air was all aflame,
Where the warrior's bloody steel on the warrior's armor came.
And still they fought and fell, where the fiery torrent rolled.
Till o'er that bloody dell shone the rising sun of gold;
Then hearts grew sick and weak, and the bravest of the brave
Grew pale, and ceased to speak: each step was on a grave.
Then courage on them fell; their foemen saw their doom;
With shout and trumpet-knell, that filled their ranks with gloom,
Down swept, with rage and power, with cannon and with shell, —

Down poured that flaming shower, and fast the
    foeman fell;
And ere that day was done the loyal banners
    waved,
And the lurid setting sun flashed o'er a country
    saved.

DRIFTING AWAY.

Drifting away to the mystical seas,
  Laden with fruit of the bright summer years;
Leaving the lone, leafless autumn to me,
  Freighted with hope, and with song, and with fears.
Drifting away to th' eternal shore,
  Laden with hopes from the years that have fled;
Leaving the wail of a sad "Nevermore;"
  Leaving the graves of the beautiful dead.

Drifting away through the tide of the years,
  Breasting the waves of the treacherous stream;
Leaving a lone, doubting watcher with tears,
  Bearing the wealth of life's midsummer dream.
Drifting away to th' eternal shore,
  Bearing the song that the early years sung;
Echoes the wail of the lone nevermore,
  Back by the winds of the autumn-night flung.

DRIFTING AWAY.

Drifting away through the daylight and dark ;
   Drifting away to the solemn unknown ;
Afloat on the river, my venturesome bark,
   Laden with hopes from the summer years flown.
Drifting away on the mystical tide ;
   Drifting alone to the eternal sea ;
Angels will wait on that echoless side,
   Guarding my bark and its treasures for me.

ON NEW YEAR'S EVE.

I wait in the dusk of the vanishing years,
  I list to the tread of their lingering feet.
Their white faces glide through a glimmer of tears,
  With waft of a melody subtle and sweet.

The beautiful years in the level, sweet light
  Of a far young moon in her languishing sway,
With glimmer of stars on their evergreen height,
  And glittering dreams of a sweet summer day.

That opulent day mid the fragrant, white year,
  That year of sweet promise that came nevermore,
But in dim, broken dreams of a summertide near,
  With perfect white blooms on a luminous shore.

ON NEW YEAR'S EVE.

Oh, that turbulent year, with never a sun!
   Oh, wildering briers with never a rose!
Oh, white, frozen faces when battles were done,
   And strange, crimson shroud of the warrior's repose.

Oh, where is the sun of those shuddering years?
   And where is the summer with never a bloom?
Oh, where is the heaven we fret with our tears?
   Oh great, weary years in the blank, starless gloom.

But the sweet, white years rolled over the pain,
   And the balm leaves trailed in the paths of the Rod;
And the brave, tried souls of our glorified slain,
   With the blooms grew fair in the summer of God.

I wait in the dusk of the shadowy years,
   And I think of the hopes and loves that have fled,
The light and the blossom that vanished in tears,
   And heaven seems near with the Beautiful Dead.

And I think this burden of crosses and cares
   Is blessed and kind when the journey is trod,
The shadow of Angels that walk unawares,
   And lead to the Calms by the River of God.

REQUIEM.

Pale rose the moon beyond the mountain side;
Pale gleams a star where Day in sorrow died;
Cold comes the wind from o'er the western sea;
Cold, lone, and dark the world is left to me.

Silent the voices that thrilled through the past;
Silent the hearts and hands oft I have clasped;
Cold are the brows that Death's pale fingers pressed,—
Cold as the snow-wreath, on high mountain crest.

Strong grows the oak beneath the wind and rain;
Strong grows the heart beneath a bitter pain;
Soft beams a star where erst the sun had set;
Calm now the face that bitter tears have wet.

Deep lie the pearls beneath the chanting waves;
Deep in the heart lie many shrouded graves;
Clasp thy pale gems, O waves of moaning sea!
Clasp, O sad heart! the loves that died to thee.

Fair are the gems in the dark ocean's cave;
Fair are the blossoms that bloom on the grave;
Pure is the dawn from night of falling rain;
Pure is the heart that *trusts* through Life's deep pain.

LENT.

I KNELT alone with my soul, my sorrowful soul,
With sins of omission and commission in long
 scroll,
While angels of fast and Lenten confession
Awaited my audible, trembling expression.
I drank the bitter lees of the soul that dares
 look
With fatal scrutiny on the unwritten book,
That clasped and hidden lies, close sealed to all
 but God, —
That book of human life, wide-open unto God.

I lifted up my prayer of passion and of loss;
To heights of God's great pity I took my weary
 cross;
I said: Of sinners and sinning I am the chief;
Not unbelief, dear Father, but perfect belief;
Yet dumb I sat and heard thy precious truth
 denied,
And walked in pleasant places, while Christs
 were crucified.

Since from the deeps of chaos came organized decree
The primal law is manifest in all, save me.

For when I knew thy truth, dear God, I spoke it not,
Or 'mid the taunting of earth voices half forgot.
The constellations sweep forever in their place;
The earth is young forever, with sweet infant grace;
The glory of this morn the primal morning saw;
The glow-worms praise Thee and know the life of thy law.
I have loved for human love: Thou art divine;
Oh, let thy smiling countenance above me shine.

When to this weary soul shall Easter morn arise?
Thou know'st my Lenten sorrow, my life sacrifice;
How often and often the bitter outweighs the sweet,
And the glowing, brimful goblet is dashed to my feet.
I keep my fast by day, I keep my watch by night;

I look through the crystal of tears, be it ever
 so light ;
I pour my soul in oblation, I yield my youth :
Oh, grant me, dear Father, forever, thy Spirit of
 Truth.

EASTER.

WHILE in the East the stars with primal splendor
  Move white and shining through the ancient skies,
A holy Presence cometh, still and tender,—
  The dawning glory, thrilled with swift surprise,
    When Christ arose.

How did He come, and with what tender message
  Will He return, this resurrection morn?
With what new joy, or with what angel presage,
  Or swelling anthem, shall the day new born
    Greet Him anew?

    With what glad psalm
Shall we forget the weary Lenten crosses,—
  The heavy watches through the awful night?
With what new gift shall Heaven replete earth's losses,
  What touch restore our blindness into sight,
    With heavenly calm?

EASTER.

   The Christ arose :
Then unto Death comes Life's new resurrection ;
 Life's awful sorrows and Death's bitter pain
Are sacred chrisms, to his own perfection,
 And Lenten sacrifice is Easter gain —
   Its toil, repose.

   From that fair home
Of many mansions, in the sunrise shining,
 With tender footfalls, noiseless by the way,
The Presence comes, with his beloved reclining,
 With tender mandate, on this Easter Day,
   Unto his own.

   Come unto me,
From out the shadow of Earth's lowly places ;
 Forth from the life so weary, hard, and plain,
The dead joys shine anew from angel faces ;
 My touch is healing on the bruised heart's
  pain,
   I come again.

EASTER.

Oh could we wait with them, in vigils keeping
    The sad nights through,
Those worn disciples, or from troubled sleeping
    Awake anew,
  And know the Lord had risen from the grave,
    What should we crave?

I think that I should ask some tender token
    From the old life,
If through the awful silence He had broken
    The mortal strife
  Still lingered in the holy atmosphere
    He brought so near.

And if upon the resurrection morning
    I once might see
The wondrous splendor o'er his features dawning,
    Although it be
  A tender presence passing swift and white
    With peace and light.

EASTER.

Beyond the need of heavy, Lenten grieving,
    The fast and cross
To the sad soul a heavenly prescience leaving
    For pain and loss ;
  To wait at sunrise by that conquered grave,
    No more I 'd crave.

Yet through this calm, sweet, hallowed Easter,
    Although unseen,
I think He comes, the blessed Guide and Master,
    In peace serene,
  His presence shining through the weary way,
    To this glad day.

And from that home of many mansions, turning,
    Her sorrow done,
Perhaps the Mary, with that earthward yearning
    For Christ the Son,
  Will listen to the pean and the psalm,
    From Heaven's own calm.

CHRISTMAS.

I WONDER, if among those heavenly places,
   The restful, holy hills that shine afar,
The children, with their Christ-like, heavenly faces,
   Will earthward turn to watch the Bethlehem star.

I wonder, if amid those mansions holy,
   The saints keep record of this gracious morn,
Or, if they sing, as sang those Shepherds lowly,
   The wondrous hymn when Christ, the Lord, was born.

Or, if the Master's best belovéd, turning
   With face and mien all tenderly benign,
To where the holy star is eastward burning,
   Will utter, "Master, lo, the olden sign!"

I wonder, if the wise, sweet, virgin mother,
   All shining white with love for her great Son,

Will tender turn to some lone, sorrowing other,
   With peace-balms till the agony be done.

I think with her the chiefest, gladdest wonder, —
   Her calm, pure eyes upon the skies afar, —
Is, though the ages roll the ages under,
   With steady light still beams the Bethlehem star.

And where will Christ be on that day, I wonder?
   Within our portals, in our open homes,
With broken bars the death-gates roll asunder,
   And softly, all unseen, the Master comes.

Will He make record of our high endeavor,
   The futile outgrowth of our gorgeous dream?
Or have they drifted to the vast forever, —
   The lofty aims that but a mirage seem?

Into this life with all its sad surprises,
   Unto the soul that walks the world alone,
Beyond the depths the glad, sweet star uprises,
   The blessed Master cometh to His own.

He comes with light, into the sad, hard places,
   He folds his loved in raiment white as snow,

He tints with life the lost, white, silent faces,
  He leadeth where the restful rivers flow.

We know beyond the glooms are shining places,
  The wondrous chorus of the heavenly sphere,
The sacred splendor of those saintly faces,
  Though all unseen, we sometimes feel it near.

Beyond the veil,. his features unrevealing,
  His tender footfalls soundless by the way,
He comes unto His own in gracious dealing,
  The joyful herald of this Christmas Day.

NEED OF ME.

One thought sublimely sweet,
   Where'er my wanderings be,
One star to guide my feet;—
   The Lord hath need of me.

When friends are cold, or far,
   Whate'er of life betide,
Thou art my guiding star;
   In Thee I still abide.

When tears on some sad face
   In lonely vale I see,
The Lord is in that place,
   Some soul has need of me.

Across the solemn tide
   The Father's mansions be;
Yet here — I will not chide, —
   The Lord hath need of me.

NEED OF ME.

When my sad soul is thrilled
   By some sweet sounding chord,
Or with deep sorrow filled,
   To dwell with Christ my Lord,

A voice serenely sweet
   In silence comes to me,
"Here, at my bleeding feet,
   I still have need of Thee."

Dear Lord, I work and wait,
   Content that 't is for Thee ;
When at thy pearly gate,
   Still, Lord, have need of me.

MY ANGEL VISITANT.

'TWILIGHT o'er the earth was stealing,
   Twilight with its golden star;
Many lamps were faintly gleaming,
   From the dusky city far;
Scarce the wild bird's wing was folded,
   Scarce was hushed his daytime song,
And each tiny blossom quivered
   As the zephyrs swept along.

Fitful flashed the golden moonbeams
   By the quiet river shore,
As I leaned me sadly dreaming, —
   Dreaming as I 've oft before;
And I heard the viewless flutter
   Of a presence strangely fair,
Without murmur, touch, or vision,
   Yet I heard and knew it there.

And I knew my angel mother,
   With her deep, unfathomed eyes,

With her saintly brow uplifted
   To the glory of the skies.
Then I hushed my gentlest breathing,
   Every wayward thought and wild,
While inaudible her blessings
   Fluttered o'er her weary child.

All the strange, sweet hours of night-time
   Lingering touches swept my brow,
With a thrill of life diviner,
   And I seem to feel it now, —
But the dawn began to quiver, —
   Dome of sapphire tipped with gold,
And the shepherds o'er the mountain
   Called the lambkins from their fold.

Gently, then, as snowy rose-leaves
   By celestial fountains fall,
Softly as the angel voices
   In their earthly missions call,
All invisible and soundless,
   Something vanished through the air,
And I nightly wait the coming,
   Down the twilight's viewless stair.

REVERIES.

Sad moans the wind this dreary December,
  On barren hills lies the desolate snow;
On my lonely hearth the flickering ember,
  'Through shadowful gleams, strange fantasies glow, —
Phantoms so strange, with mystical faces, —
  With mild, pleading eyes, from years that have gone, —
While firelight gleams through desolate places,
  And wintry winds moan, with low, mocking tone.

Sad wails the wind its wild legends telling, —
  Dying the light on the desolate hearth;
Borne through the night, in loud chorus swelling,
  Are dirges of death and anthems of birth;
Pale rise the guests from the whit'ning ashes,
  Speak with the breath of the soul-haunting wind;

I know their forms, by dim ember-flashes,
   Star-gleams and moon-gleams through half open blind.

Sweet are the tales of years that have vanished,
   Beautiful years that can never return;
Beautiful hopes that cannot be banished,
   In the heavens of the soul their fires will burn;
Soul speaks to soul through years long departed,
   Distance is swept by sweet mem'ry aside,
A word resurrects the long silent-hearted,
   We walk once again by dear ones who died.

O wind of the night, O flickering ember,
   What are thy sounds or thy faces to me?
What are the psalms of this dreary December?
   What of the things that are not, or that be?
Tenderest poems unwritten nor spoken,
   Beautiful visions forever unsaid,
Links of a love forever unbroken,
   Wafts from the souls of my beautiful dead.

REPROACH.

If the bird thou hast cherished
   Escapes from thy hand,
  Impatient to flit,
   O'er wild, sunlit land,
  On high cliff to sit,
Where the wild chamois perished,
    Would'st thou blame or deride him,
    Whatever betide him?
     Thou would'st speak of the bird
     With tenderest word.
     Would *I* were a bird.

If the bird proudly perished,
   On far, rocky height,
  With deep, cruel stain,
   In cold, starless night,
  Where pity is vain, —
Bird that thou dearly cherished, —
    But he plumed for the far sky,
    The cloud and the star high,
     Would'st thou grant him one tear,

In strange atmosphere?
Would *I* were thus dear.

If the rose thou hast cherished,
　Uplifts to the sun
　Her sweet, blushing face,
　By his soft beams won,—
Rose with tender grace,
By those bright arrows perished,
　　Would'st speak of pride supremely,
　　Or glances unseemly?
　　　Ah no, O noble rose,
　　　In glorious repose.
　　Would *I* were a rose.

If a star, through the ether
　Should fall from the sky,
Adown through the night,
　From its mansion high,
With swift, trailing light—
Lost on the wild, dreary heather,
　　Would'st thou turn in deep scorning,
　　And laugh with the morning?
　　　Ah no, O lovely star,
　　　Wandering afar.
　　Would *I* were a star.

ANNA SNOW. (SONG.)

I stood where the cheek of love grew pale,
    Where the hopes of years lay low,
Where Death had kissed the marble brow
    Of little Anna Snow.
Little Anna, darling Anna,
    Thou art sleeping now,
And the silent stars are weeping
    O'er thy snowy brow.

I stood where the moonlight dim and still,
    Lay on her golden hair;
She clasped her lily hands and said
    Her quiet, evening prayer.
Little Anna, darling Anna,
    Thou art sleeping now,
And the silent stars are weeping
    O'er thy snowy brow.

She died, and now I'm sad and lone,
    And often I long to go,

For my wearied heart is in the grave
With little Anna Snow.
Good-by, good-by, darling Anna,
Thou art sleeping now,
And the silent stars are weeping
O'er thy snowy brow.

ALMOST.

Some time, amid the pauses of our care and strife,
Comes a solemn yearning for a nobler life —
For some deeper purpose, for a light divine,
O'er our darkened pathway some pure star to shine.

And we almost catch the meaning life portrays;
Almost lose, in adoration, life's dark days;
Almost see the end triumphant drawing nigh —
See the signs of victory bending from the sky;

Almost grasp the secret of eternal things;
Almost see the gleaming of immortal wings;
Almost hear the answer to our longing cry;
Almost know the wherefore to our ceaseless why;

Almost —— But hereafter, O glad soul of mine,
Reap the full fruition of this cross of thine;

Know what now but darkly through the glass
    appears ;
Find the perfect answer to thy woe and tears.

Courage, then, faint-hearted pilgrim! With the
    blest,
At life's weary ending, cometh peaceful rest!
After life's long supplication, heaven is sweet!
After life's great tribulation, joy complete!

AFTERWARD.

ORION hid in a phantom sky,
   Where clouds rolled up from the southern seas;
The moon like a pallid ghost slid by
   The shrouded path of the Pleiades;—
One single star on the mountain height,
   Serene and fair from its heavenly goal,
A steady gleam flung over the night,
   Like thought of God to a troubled soul.

The swift simoon swung over the plain
   In sullen wrath his withering breath;
The blank sky rifted a leaden rain;
   My rose blooms swooned in pallor of death;—
Like waft from the realm of immortal bloom,
   A fragrance stole transcendingly sweet.
A strange white flower entangled the gloom,
   The hushed wind flung at my waiting feet.

My bird that thrilled the luminous dawn,
   With song too glad for the nether years,

Evanished to thrill the glorified morn,
   In sunlit space of the swinging spheres;—
My tiny, brown bird trilled all day long,
   A melody low and tenderly sweet,
A free, glad life breathed into the song,
   A sweet, white path enchanted my feet.

A lofty soul a solitude sought,
   A tangled, bloomless venturesome maze;
A fearless bark on a sea of thought,
   A trackless waste of wildering ways;
But step by step and in thought by thought,
   The intricate chaos safely trod,
For, through those splendid purposes wrought
   A love of truth and a thought of God.

The darkest cloud embosoms a star;
   The wildest grief imprisons a balm;
The storms that sweep and battle afar,
   May waft a breath from heaven's own calm;
And while aweary we turn the page
   That slow reveals God's infinite plan,
We catch a gleam of the Golden Age,
   The grand ideal of the Perfect Man.

THE WEDDED LIFE.

Thou of the loyal heart,
   Tender and kind,
Life of my life a part,
   Mine, as I 'm thine;
Deep in thy peerless soul,
   Fountains of truth;
Years will unchanging roll,
   Youth of my youth.

Dear as the morning light,
   Free from all care;
Dear as the starry night,
   Pure and as fair:
Close to thy faithful heart
   Tenderly fold;
Love of God's love a part
   Cannot grow cold.

Thou of the noble life,
   Living for me,

I am thy trusting wife,
    Loving but thee:
Time brings no change in me,
    Death cannot part;
God will be kind to thee,
    Heart of my heart.

CHRISTMAS HYMN.

Peace, peace o'er the ransomed world,
   Living, flowing, and free;
Peace, peace on the shining hills,
   Peace o'er land and sea:
Calm through the dawn holy
   Blessings flutter and fall;
Peace, peace as a river,
   For Heaven is over all.

Love, love o'er the ransomed world,
   Blending earth and sky;
Love, love from the angel songs
   That cannot change or die:
Soft through the light dawning
   Angel ministries fall;
Love, love as a fountain,
   For God is over all.

Joy, joy o'er the ransomed world,
   Sung from harp and choir;

Joy, through chant and pæan rung,
   From dome to flashing spire:
Glorious, glad tidings,
   Good-will and peace, the call:
Joy, joy as the morning,
   For Christ is over all.

TRUST.

Does life's strange and wayward journey
    Aimless seem, —
  A wayward, causeless dream,
    Where deep woes betide,
    Where hopes are crucified?
Beyond our vision's ken God works our weal,
    Forever near;
Amid life's pain and mystery, why feel
    One fear?

  Should our loved be early taken,
    While we grieve
  For life's young, withered leaves —
    With soul-anguished cry,
    "Father, tell us why," —
From the chill waters and life's wasted bloom,
    Under the rod,
While groping blindly through the dusk and
    gloom,
    Trust God.

Are we seeking, bowed with sorrows,
All alone,
That undiscovered zone,
By the sacred cross
We may bear our loss.
Why fear what Christ, the holiest,
Has borne before?
He leaveth us, the lone, the lowliest,
No more.

MY HEAVENLY FRIEND.

HAVE you forgotten me, my best beloved,
    My own, I wonder?
Scarce three lone years agone were our close paths
    Riven asunder.

Have you known how I sought you, precious one;
    My true, my dearest?
And deemed, when midnight glooming filled my room,
    Your presence nearest?

Did my wild anguish thrill you, ransomed one,
    In heaven's repose;
Or, when my Woe with Peace was reconciled,
    Glad pæans rose?

When you were dying, peerless one, you called me,
    Like one off afar;

I could not pass the gate, although you told me
    'T was half ajar.

The inmost temple of our being is
    The soul's sacred shrine;
Death rent in twain one shadowy veil between
    Your true life and mine.

Only one lance to be shivered, saintly one;
    One veil rent in twain;
On that last, mighty day I shall clasp you,
    My soul's own soul again.

RECOMPENSE.

Shall we seek in early springtide
 To bind the golden corn?
Shall we seek repose of even
 In flush of early dawn?
Shall we look for gleaming harvests
 Through brown, unbroken fields?
Shall we garner fruits in summer
 Which autumn only yields?

Shall we walk the fresh, green highlands,
 Or on the pure, calm hills?
Shall we drink from crystal fountains,
 And bathe in fragrant rills?
Shall we list to heavenward music,
 Yet breathe to earth no song?
Shall we rest in high, cool places,
 While weak ones labor long?

Let us break the sod in springtime,
 And sow our scanty seed;

Though we weep o'er vacant caskets,
  And wait in patient need;
Though we wait in dark, sad places,
  And plead one drop of rain,
God is God of seed and harvest,
  And labor is not vain.

Should we reach the golden hill-tops,
  And glimpse the rising sun,
Should we hear from sacred voices,
  "Loved one, well done, well done!"
May we turn to lone, low valleys,
  To those in shadow still,
May we bring sweet breath of mountain,
  And pure, sweet draughts from rill.

May we share with bitter sorrow
  Our unforgotten pain;
May we wait by silent watchers
  That watch and wait in vain.
If we sow, we shall be reapers,
  And pain is not all pain;
There's recompense in sacrifice,
  And loss is greatest gain.

WHERE CAN THE SOUL FIND REST?

Where can the soul find rest,
  Oh sainted one?
Where are the peaceful shores of the blest,
  Life's labor done?
Where is the laurel crown,
  Where yield the cross?
Where the full recompense,
  Counting our loss?

Where art *thou* resting now,
  Beautiful saint?
Whence the peace on thy radiant brow?
  Hear my complaint.
Where fell *thy* burden down,
  Where ceased thy pain?
When hushed thy griefs and tears,
  Falling like rain?

Where thy pure dwelling-place,
  True, deathless friend?

WHERE CAN THE SOUL FIND REST?

Come, let me gaze on thy heavenly face:
  One token send.
Where can my soul repose,
  Striving no more,
Where find its home with thee, —
  Heaven's blesséd shore?

Over the river cold
  Can they forget?
Friend of our childhood's time,
  Come to us yet.
Oh, come to my weary soul,
  Longing for rest,
Tell of the summer land
  Home of the blest.

Tell us to work and wait,
  Watch, and be strong;
Life, with its labor and fleeting hours,
  Cannot be long.
All of its ills and pains
  Patient endure;
Faithful our God shall be;
  Heaven is secure.

UNDER THE SNOW.

Under the frozen turf,
    Silent and cold,
Wintry winds drifting snow
    Over the wold.

Hands meekly folded down
    Over his breast.
Lost to life's fitful way,
    God giveth rest.

Cold are the stars to-night, —
    Colder his brow;
Over his flowerless grave
    Tearless I bow.

Death on his warrior brow,
    Frosty and white,
Death from his glorious eye
    Quenching the light.

One link is left to us, —
  God's tender soul,
Folding thy soul in peace, —
  Death's billows roll.

Earth-worn and weary, now,
  Knelt by thy grave;
Death has no fears to us, —
  God's love will save.

COMPENSATION.

Ambitious, eager soul,
Impatient of control,
And hidden chains wherewith we 're darkly bound,
Seeking faultless treasures,
Grasping unknown pleasures,
And faulting much for recompense unfound;

Our toil without fruition,
In realms of our transition,
Are Life's instalments for the palm and crown;
Record no burden loss,
Our Saviour bore the cross:
Along the heavenward way earth's bleak hills frown.

Our wearying and our loss,
Our Calvary and our cross,
Are shadows of that love too great to know;
Redeemed through sacrifice,
The fettered soul may rise:
Why languish we while thitherward we go?

A DAY OF GLADNESS.

The light wind lifts the tasseled corn,
   And ripples in the golden sheaves,
And o'er the wide sward, warm and brown,
   The lustrous orange swings its leaves.

The constant roses bud and bloom,
   The lilies gleam along the way,
And all the fair land glows beneath
   The glory of this perfect day.

The lowing herds browse on the hill,
   Or eager seek the cool, still stream;
The bleating of some distant flocks
   Falls on the sense, like some dim dream.

And high athwart the ether space
   The wild bird carols to the sun;
And drowsy, golden-crested bees
   Hum softly through the pastures dun.

A DAY OF GLADNESS.

The azure sea smiles to the sky;
   The azure sky smiles on the sea;
The air is glad with laugh and song;
   The warm, sweet sunlight falls on me.

And I am glad, oh wide, sweet earth,
   For sometimes through the mist of tears
I saw this landscape and this sea,
   Adown the vista of the years.

I will be glad; for true as thou,
   Oh warm, sweet earth, and wide, sweet sea,
A soul knelt at my soul's white feet,
   With love that answered love to me.

I will be glad: the tropic sun
   Shines on the land this perfect day,
And orange buds and orange blooms
   Lie white athwart my sunny way.

DEAD.

The white mist falls from stony skies,
    And shivers all the world's blank space;
And through the mists of yearning eyes
    I look upon a still, white face.

The sad, white roses scent the gloom;
    The sobbing lily droops its head;
One awful stillness fills the room;
    I gaze upon my perfect dead.

The frightened herds have left the hill;
    The birds have left the shuddering sky;
The distant, bleating flocks are still;
    The heavens are dumb to every cry.

And oh, those perfect lips are dumb,
    And stony dumb is everything,
And nevermore sweet words shall come
    From those shut lips, my love, my king.

There is no light upon the sky,
  And awful sorrows toss the sea;
The earth is thrilled with one full cry,
  Oh, bring my love, my king, to me!

ONE.

You may gather all the sweet roses,
   Wild roses of sunny blown snow,
Bright pansies of gold and of purple,
   And all the white lilies that grow;
Sweet blossoms of garden and wayside,
   Flowers tinted of suns and of snows,
But leave me, O beautiful gleaner,
   My dainty, pink bud of a rose.

You may take the world and its splendor
   Of kingdoms and purples and crowns;
The cruel, wide world, and surrender
   Your soul to its smiles and its frowns;
And, dazzled with fame and with fortune,
   May ring your proud name to the dome,
But leave me the still, sunny places,
   The sunny, sweet faces of home.

You may win the proud and the noble
   With vows that are tender and sweet;

ONE.

The world in its passionate splendor
   May kneel at your conquering feet;
It may come with gifts and oblations,
   Rare treasures of land and of sea,
But leave, in your glory and gladness,
   My loyal, one lover, to me.

THE LOST LOVE.

Was it the gold of the dead leaves falling?
   Was it the sheen of the sunset sea?
Was it the voice of the night-bird calling
   Low, through the dim, sweet meadows to me?

Was it the spray from the bright waves blowing?
   Was it a sail on the flashing tide?
Was it a star through the zenith going?
   Was it the soul of my fair, dead bride?

Linger with me, O calm of the gloaming,
   Lull me with voices so sweet and far;
Waft her white robes, O light breezes roaming;
   Tint her long tresses, O moonbeam and star.

Was it a dream of the sunset glory?
   Was it the flutter of dead leaves near?
Only a fancy, the old, sweet story?
   Fancy, the voices so tender and clear?

Only the mist of the blank sky falling;
  Only the flash of the wild, white sea;
Only the sob of the night-wind calling;
  Never my lost love coming to me.

RESPITE.

When wearied of futile endeavor,
   When, baffled, I sink in the strife,
In vain search the pledges of labor
   Or solve the deep problems of life,
I turn with the awful unanswered
   From conflict of Right and of Wrong,
I wonder if God has forgotten,
   And victory dwells with the strong:
I question the Infinite forces,
   The systems and cycles untrod,
And trace through the absolute vastness
   The Infinite purpose of God.

I watch the emblazoned battalions
   Of stars wheeling silently on,
The Heavens in their marvelous glory,
   The Earth and the splendor thereon;
I marvel the vast incompleteness,
   When cycles of ages are trod,
And long for the final revealing
   Of Thought, the creation of God;

RESPITE.

With thrill of the love everlasting,
  With waft from the fateful undone,
With joy the vast purpose fulfilling,
  I turn to the mighty unwon.

I know, though the ages evanish,
  And evil and darkness withstand,
The Heavens gather new constellations,
  Forever creations expand ;
I think, with a swift exultation,
  The forces of Truth shall avail,
And Peace, like a new benediction,
  Shall vanquish the hosts that prevail ;
I smile at the futile endeavor,
  With eager soul turned to the strife ;
Abide the sure harvest of labor,
  And solve the true problems of life.

THE USES OF LIFE.

Should we grasp one truth profound,
   Should we hold some region vast
   Of the venerated Past,
Should we mount to height sublime, by mortals
     yet unfound,
   Should we enter some temple untrod —
   Sacred to secrets of God:
If we yield no answer to Humanity's great claim,
We have thought our thoughts in vain.

Should our souls be stern and strong,
   Dauntless in the battle's heat,
   Undismayed by swift defeat:
If we strengthen not the weary, if we right no
     wrong,
   If we crush not false with iron hand,
   Bind not truth with golden band,
Give no courage to the doubting, to no loss our
     gain —
Our strength, our power, is vain.

If by ceaseless, strong desire,
   Underneath some bitter cross,
   Counting selfhood utter loss :
If through agony untold, one soul has come up
      higher,
   Yet calls not through that shadowy place,
   Pleading from its calm, white place,
Reaching down through depths of conquered pain,
We have climbed the heights in vain.

Should we hear, or almost hear,
   Hymns by mortal thought unknown,
   Saints have sung by shining throne —
Hear the infinite, sweet chorus of the swinging
      spheres :
   If we knew or if we ALMOST knew,
   Yet led no shrinking traveler through
Portals dim of doubt, to pathways pure, and
      high, and plain,
We have heard and known in vain.

ANSWERED.

O SOUL of the mountain! O soul of the sea!
Soul of the valley, and all things that be,
Come thou and whisper thy secret to me.

O solitude pregnant with woe and with weal,
All that a mortal may know or may feel —
Language to utter what God may reveal!

O vastness of space! O freedom of thought!
Ages on ages thy being hath wrought;
Prophets and sages thy wonders have sought.

O silent cathedral! O temple untrod!
Pure as the breath from the spirit of God;
Soul of the sunlight that falls on the sod.

O spirit of goodness! O soul of the true!
Soul of all matter that is or that grew;
Tell me the secret to grow and to do.

ANSWERED.

I listened and waited in silence and prayer,
Flung from my spirit its cross of despair,
Soul spoke to soul through the measureless air,

O soul! little soul springing up from the sod,
Bless thou the blessing, and bless thou the rod.
Goodness and truth is the spirit of God.

The mountain, the valley, the grass and the tree,
The light and the air, all space and the sea
Speak through the silence that speaketh to thee.

To grow is to wait and to watch and to pray,
Seeking in silence, by night and by day.
Law is the secret and truth is the way.

Thy life is to be, to do, and to bless;
Immortal the goal and true happiness, —
HE DOETH THE MOST WHO LOVETH THE BEST.

PERADVENTURE.

When some sweet hope is defeated
   And lofty endeavor seems vain,
And life a subtle mystery
   Of wrong, injustice, and pain:
When strifes and futile contentions
   Their forces around us draw,
I long for a new dispensation,
   A new revelation of law.
I think of the new evolutions
   Of life that is sadder than death
The heavens seem darkened forever,
   And my prayer is a baffled breath.

Echoes of strife surge around us,
   And I look in vain for a sign
Of Christ's sweet kingdom begotten,
   Of teachings and tokens benign;
I think of the gentle high precepts,
   Of Jesus — so slow to condemn —
And a tender thought sweeps o'er me,
   With the thrill of a sweet amen;

And I know should He walk the wayside
  Or stand in the holiest place,
There would only a look of pity
  Shine over his eloquent face;
His presence bring peace to passion,
  His touch would be balm to the smart
Of the cruel and pitiless bruises
  That fall to the aching heart.

Perhaps in his gentle silence
  He would stoop and write on the ground,
While the hosts that spurn and revile us
  Would pass with never a sound;
Perhaps the one that *seems* vilest
  Would stand with the Christ alone,
With never a voice to scorn her,
  Nor hand to cast her a stone.
Though outrage, strife, and confusion
  The forces of Truth shall withdraw;
I know that God moves with a purpose,
  There is Life and Love in his law.

THERE IS NO LOSS.

There is no loss!
For, when my rose her snowy blossom swung
In royal beauty from her emerald throne,
The sun's sweet love-light on her pure heart shone,
While, leaf by leaf, he stole her life away;
The air grew more delicious day by day,
Through subtile incense that she, dying, flung;
And one — deep dreamer — when her life had flown,
The true rose-life held sacred in his own.

There is no loss!
For, when my birdie plumed her golden wings
To cleave the splendor of the sunset skies;
When radiant Summer, woed by Autumn's sighs,
Her wealth of sweetness regally she flung,
My birdie's pinions flash, through spice trees, swung

By tropic winds, and by some opal stream she sings,
Her song grown sweeter, more divinely clear,
Through sunlit space of some glad atmosphere.

There is no loss!
For, when I loved, with love beyond all friend,
And skies grew dark through sobs of Autumn rain,
And sweet hope died, and joy turned bitter pain —
Life one sad round of parting and of tears,
And slow days crept to months and weary years —
Joy learned with grief in harmony to blend,
And Sorrow reconciled with Peace sublime,
Then Love triumphant conquered space and time.

There is no loss!
For, though one tender Spring, a pure, white soul —
Life's solemn mystery but just begun —
Forth from my clasping arms — a sinless one —
Evanished through gates of immortal flowers

That shut the viewless angel-realm from ours;
  I know, that over where the death-tides roll,
From saintly calm of everlasting hill
A pure, white soul is waiting for me still.

UNUTTERED THOUGHTS.

How sad, yet kingly it must be for souls,
   In lone, deep silence of unuttered thought,
To enter realms so vast and unexplored,
    Where age on age the light of truth hath
       brought;
And stand with dumb lips on the verge
       Of seen and unseen things,
       Like crownless, exiled kings.

How sadly fated for those sealed lips
   To bind the secrets of the great To Be;
With mute soul grasp the mighty unrevealed,
   Like some deep river shut from hungry sea;
To dash against those silent walls,
       That wordless height to reach
       Of great, unuttered speech.

How grandly desolate that prophet soul
   That sends no voice across the vast abyss
Of solitude that girds each human soul,
   Like far off world that sends no light to this;

To dwell amid the great unsaid
    Like bird on Alpine height,
    Or star in polar night.

On that glad day, when from those mute, shut lips
    The seal of silence shall be rolled away,
And peals of joy break o'er the soul's eclipse,
    As sang the stars at dawn of one glad day;
When souls shall sing the great unsung,
    And touch with living fire
    The poet's sacred lyre;

How wondrous sweet will that glad anthem be,
    For age on age in raptured silence bound,
And vale and hill, the mountain and the sea,
    And earth and heaven shall list to that sweet sound;
O soul of great unuttered things,
    O silent voice of fate,
    The dumb souls longing wait!

PROPHECY.

O SILENT night! O weary, pallid moon,
   Forever sailing on thy shoreless quest,
Shall not the morning sun arise full soon,
   And life and love fulfill the soul's unrest?

O dumb, relentless night! O speechless skies!
   Hast thou no voice to break the dead white calm,
No kindling soul-fires from all-seeing eyes,
   Nor presage of diviner song and psalm?

The ancient, shining stars are all alight;
   The shadows lift along the mountain range;
A sound is surging through the awful night,
   With trembling prelude of prophetic change.

The slow, dumb ages quicken into life,
   And nations list the chorus from afar;
Fair Peace shall dawn on this uncertain strife,
   And Freedom shine from out the morning star.

O waiting world, forever in thy place!
  The Right shall triumph over shame and wrong;
New joy shall sweep athwart thy troubled face,
  Thy vigils break with victory and song.

ON THE SUMMIT.

Weary has been the way, and oh, so long
   The sunburnt path beneath our stumbling feet;
The small, brown linnet trilled a faint, sweet song,
   The white bay glimmered through the blinding heat.

Sometimes, above the dusty, dead-ripe grass,
   The palm trees lifted shadows cool and deep,
And slow, sweet breezes touching, as they pass,
   Our fevered foreheads with the balm of sleep.

Sometimes a mirage, fair and shining far,
   Allured our footfalls unto bitter ways,
And cruel skies shot down a wayward star,
   And all the world grew dark unto our gaze.

Sometimes a vineyard, cool and long and wide,
   The drooping fruitage sweet with rosy wine,

And harvest fields, afoam on either side,
  With eager sweetness filled the summer shine.

And meadow waters laved our restless feet,
  And dark, high rivers balmed our burning eyes,
And far, green hilltops, lifted dim and sweet
  With haunting dreams of some new paradise.

Some distant notes were all our thought could know
  Of perfect cadence of the song divine, —
A starlit glimmer on a crest of snow,
  Whose thrilling splendors from the summit shine.

With weary steps forever faltering on,
  With weary eyes forever on the hill,
Through weary hours, when moon and stars were gone,
  One mighty impulse moved us onward still.

Triumphant on the summit hills aglow —
  The radiant day effulgent, high and wide, —
The great, new future rising to the flow
  Of nobler hopes and truth's incoming tide.

ON THE SUMMIT.

To breathe the pure air on the hills divine, —
  To grasp the truth that bids the soul be free —
To make the splendor and the perfume mine —
  This is the glory of the life to be.

STRANDED.

Only the gray, cold sky,
  Only the gray, cold sea;
One white sail drifting by,
  Freighted with naught for me.

Only the sad wind's sigh,
  The sea-gull's startled flight,
One frail boat stranded nigh;—
  Alone I stand on the height.

What have you lost for me,
  Boat of the wild, lone shore?
Lost in the sorrowful sea,
  Never to find them more?

What do you bear from me?
  Treasures I've sought in vain?
Phantom bird of the sea,
  Out on the pathless main?

STRANDED.

What do you say to me?
   What mystic, secret lore,
Voice of the solemn sea,
   By this wild, haunted shore?

No gleam, O gray, cold sky,
   No gem, O gray, cold sea;
One white sail gliding by,
   Leaving no friend for me.

DESTINY.

The summer will bloom into roses,
  And laughter will follow your tears;
I linger alone in the shadows
  That fell from the beautiful years.

The autumn will shine into harvests,
  The grapes will hang purple with wine,
The lark will sing high in the meadow;
  The shadow forever is mine.

The mountain shall lean to the valley,
  And billows flash foam from the sea,
And white ships ride safe into harbor, —
  This phantom still lingers with me.

They will stand in their old, bright places,
  The valley, the hillside and sea;
I turn to the desolate faces
  Of doubts, that are still haunting me.

You will sigh and be glad on the morrow,
  You will love and laugh and be free,
With never a thought of the shadow
  That lingers forever with me.

And time shall make level the mountains,
  And rocks shall dissolve into sand,
And seas driven outward and downward,
  Shall pledge a new highway of land.

And moons shall waver and darken
  Alone, among milky white bars;
And meteors flash from the zenith,
  And skies rain a shiver of stars.

This phantom has life everlasting,
  It is heaven and hell unto me,
Though æons of new constellations
  Are lost in an infinite sea.

BEAUTIFUL LINKS.

I caught a sigh from the golden west,
   Where the royal Day was dying,
A crimson dart through the purple vest
   Of clouds, on her great heart lying.

An eagle flew from the mountain crest,
   And swung in the golden ether,
A crimson stain on his silver breast,
   A crimson plume on the heather.

A white sail flashed where the golden sea
   Swept the robes of Daylight trailing;
A homesick song floated far to me
   From hearts with the hope light failing.

A mist crept over our longing eyes,
   When we knew our saint was going;
The Reaper waited in glad surprise
   The Sower's sorrowful sowing.

BEAUTIFUL LINKS.

The subtle changes of Life and Death,
   Love and joy, or pain and grieving,
A summer dream, an autumn breath,
   The clasp of friends we are leaving,

Are mystic links in the endless chain
   Of the infinite spheres of Being,
And hopes grow on that are early slain,
   In realms beyond our dim seeing.

The Day that died in the golden west
   Still flings its marvelous glory;
The eagle that swung from the mountain crest
   Has tinted a poet's story.

The sail that gleamed in the golden west
   When the royal Day was dying,
Has anchored afar with jeweled crest,
   Amid gems and sea-pearls lying.

The friend that vanished through mist and tears,
   With a love that faltered never,
Will crown the life of the weary years,
   The beautiful, vast forever.

IMMORTAL LIFE.

I stood on the mountain pure and high;
Gray vapors were blending sea and sky.

The shadowy mist crept o'er the sun,
The land, and the sea, and sky were one.

The mystical mountains, pure and cold,
To my waiting soul their secrets told.

And listening long and waiting well,
Inaudible voices rose and fell,

And over the sea where white mists hung,
A wonderful ship in vision swung.

The masts and the spars were burnished gold,
Upheld in the vapor's phantom fold.

O beautiful ship on yon dim sea,
Oh, bringest thou treasures vast to me?

IMMORTAL LIFE.

Some radiant gem from far, fair realm,
O beautiful ship, with golden helm?

Or anchorest thou, to wait for me,
This mystical port to a fairer sea?

I gazed on the ship of molten gold;
Inaudible sounds the secret told.

It floated away from mortal sight —
A luminous path of heavenward light.

Away and beyond the mist and the sea,
The beautiful ship is waiting me.

"IS IT UPHILL ALL THE WAY?"

Is it uphill all the wildering way?
   No; there are rests along the weary steep,
And level highlands where cool breezes stray,
   And strains of music lull to dreamful sleep.

With wounded feet the flinty paths I trace;
   To sunless crags I lift my yearning eyes;
The damp winds sweep my lifted, eager face,
   And rainfalls flash from dumb, relentless skies.

Yes, baffled and blinded, I climb the hill,
   And battle with winds under sullen skies, —
But somewhere the waters are cool and still,
   And shining pastures flushed with summer dyes.

If I should stumble 'neath my heavy load,
   Or falter in some barren, sunburnt place,
An angel hand shall smooth the uphill road,
   And angel calms shall light thy troubled face.

Shall I gain the summit and stand at last
   With tattered garments and torn, empty hands?
No; on the hills are mansions fair and vast,
   And heritage of shining harvest lands.

www.ingramcontent.com/pod-product-compliance
Lightning Source LLC
Chambersburg PA
CBHW030315170426
43202CB00009B/1005